Sunflakes
Poems for Children

SELECTED BY
Lilian Moore

ILLUSTRATED BY
Jan Ormerod

Clarion Books
New York

In memory of Carl,
the big brother with whom I shared my childhood.

Clarion Books
a Houghton Mifflin Company imprint
215 Park Avenue South, New York, NY 10003
Copyright © 1992 by Lilian Moore
Illustrations copyright © 1992 by Jan Ormerod
All rights reserved.
For information about permission to reproduce selections from
this book, write to Permissions, Houghton Mifflin Company, 2
Park Street, Boston, MA 02108.
Printed in Hong Kong

Library of Congress Cataloging-in-Publication Data
Sunflakes : poems for children / selected by Lilian Moore ;
illustrated by Jan Ormerod.
p. cm.
Summary; A collection of poems about universal childhood experiences.
ISBN 0-395-58833-2
1. Children's poetry, American. [1. American poetry —
Collections.] I. Moore, Lilian. II. Ormerod, Jan, ill.
PS586.3.S86 1992   90-23760
811.008'09282 — dc20   CIP
                                                 AC

IMS 10 9 8 7 6 5 4 3 2 1

CONTENTS

POEM TIME

Children are lucky if they have poems in their lives. They are being nourished in a very special way.

Children start out looking at the world very much as poets do, with a fresh curiosity as if everything were new — as indeed it is to the young child. They are adventuresome with language in the same spirit poets are — taking pleasure in rhythm, in playfulness with words, in unexpected word happenings.

The language of children often has the expressiveness and directness of poetry. A teacher who asked her kindergartners, "What is slow? What is quiet? What is deep?" did not get responses like "Quiet as a mouse" or "Slow as molasses." These clichés come later in life. Instead, the children said, "Quiet as you cut cotton. Slow as a new tooth coming. Deep as a giant."

What happens to this closeness of the young child and the poet? Too often, as the child grows older, this spontaneity goes underground.

But poems in the life of the child can be like the dowsing sticks that are said to find underground streams. They help children to stay in touch with the poets they really are. And because poems are more than just arrangements of words, they help children to grow in all the ways that poets offer them — in the power to connect with the feelings of others; to hear the music of language; to see the details in the world around them more vividly, more truthfully.

It is easier than ever before to make poems part of a child's life. Many fine poets have been writing for children for some time now. This collection contains the work of more than forty such poets. They speak in different voices but they speak to children from remembered childhood.

There is much sensory pleasure here in poems with the feel of wind and rain and sun, the turning of the day and the changing of the seasons.

There is everyday fun to be shared, too, in poems that play merrily with such ideas as the strange ways of sneakers and sneezes or the pleasures of puddles and gooseberry jam.

Many of these poets are concerned about the fears and worries of childhood. What does it feel like to be lost? Or when a pet dies? We understand, the poets tell the children.

The last section in this anthology is an imagination stretcher. "If only I could stand/still enough, long enough/with my arms in the air/I'm sure I could become a tree." Such is one poet's fantasy. "If sunlight fell like snowflakes . . ." he also muses. These are poems that might well encourage children to play their own poem games of *If*.

The poems in this collection have been chosen with the young school child — and the "almost-ready pre-schooler" — in mind. Many poems seem to ask to be heard again and again, and even poems not fully understood at first can become accessible and beloved in time.

Poems come from the sensibilities of poets — their humor, their exuberance, their gentleness — and they are meant *most of all* to be enjoyed, by the adult who reads them aloud and the child who listens.

There is no special voice for reading poems and there need be no special time.

Poem time is every day — any time — *now*.

Lilian Moore

I AM VERY FOND OF BUGS—

Bugs

I am very fond of bugs.
I kiss them
And I give them hugs.

Karla Kuskin

Hey, Bug!

Hey, bug, stay!
Don't run away.
I know a game that we can play.

I'll hold my fingers very still
and you can climb a finger-hill.

No, no.
Don't go.

Here's a wall — a tower, too,
a tiny bug town, just for you.
I've a cookie. You have some.
Take this oatmeal cookie crumb.

Hey, bug, stay!
Hey, bug!
Hey!

Lilian Moore

Song of the Bugs

Some bugs pinch
And some bugs creep
Some bugs buzz themselves to sleep
Buzz Buzz Buzz Buzz
This is the song of the bugs.

Some bugs fly
When the moon is high
Some bugs make a light in the sky
Flicker, flicker firefly
This is the song of the bugs.

Margaret Wise Brown

The Tickle Rhyme

"Who's that tickling my back?" said the wall.
    "Me," said a small
Caterpillar. "I'm learning
To crawl."

Ian Serraillier

Glowworm

Never talk down to a glowworm —
Such as *What do you knowworm?*
How's it down belowworm?
Guess you're quite a slowworm.
No. Just say

Helloworm!

David McCord

7 LIKE TO LOOK IN PUDDLES—

One Misty, Moisty Morning

One misty, moisty morning,
When cloudy was the weather,
There I met an old man
Clothed all in leather.
He began to compliment
And I began to grin,
"How-do-you-do,"
And "how-do-you-do,"
And "how-do-you-do, again!"

Mother Goose

Puddles

I like to look in puddles —
when I smile
they smile,
when I laugh
they laugh,
and when I cry
they don't mind getting wet.

Frank Asch

I Like It When It's Mizzly

I like it when it's mizzly
and just a little drizzly
so everything looks far away
and make-believe and frizzly.

I like it when it's foggy
and sounding very froggy.
I even like it when it rains
on streets and weepy windowpanes
and catkins in the poplar tree
and *me*.

Aileen Fisher

Rhyme

I like to see a thunder storm,
     A dunder storm,
        A blunder storm,
I like to see it, black and slow,
Come stumbling down the hills.

I like to hear a thunder storm,
     A plunder storm,
        A wonder storm,
Roar loudly at our little house
And shake the window sills!

Elizabeth Coatsworth

Storm

In a storm,
the wind talks
with its mouth open.
It yells around corners
with its eyes shut.
It bumps into itself
and falls over a roof
and whispers
OH . . . Oh . . . oh. . . .

Adrien Stoutenburg

It Rained in the Park Today

I'm ready
for my snack
and bed

Without a wash,
without
a soak,
a scrub, a spray,
a tingly rub,
without a bath —

Not in a tub!

Today,
instead,
(at twelve o'clock)
the whole first grade
and all the flowers
took our showers
in the park.

We cupped our mouths
to catch the drops
as waxy tulips
fill their cups

and as the shivery willows do,
we washed our hair
with rain shampoo!

Then holding hands
we made a train
and headed
(full steam)
towards the Zoo

where the sun
came out,
and showered, too,

and here's
the rainbow
that I drew!

So hold the soap
and save the scrub.

But since
(I see)
you've filled the tub
just let me float
until I quack —

which means
this duckling
wants her snack!
Judith Thurman

The Muddy Puddle

I am sitting
In the middle
Of a rather Muddy
Puddle,
With my bottom
Full of bubbles
And my rubbers
Full of Mud,

While my jacket
And my sweater
Go on slowly
Getting wetter
As I very
Slowly settle
To the Bottom
Of the Mud.

And I find that
What a person
With a puddle
Round his middle
Thinks of mostly
In the muddle
Is the Muddi-
Ness of Mud.

Dennis Lee

ME AND POTATO CHIPS—

Street Song

O, I have been walking
with a bag of potato chips,
me and potato chips
munching along,

Walking alone
eating potato chips,
big old potato chips,
crunching along,

walking along
munching potato chips,
me and potato chips
lunching along.

Myra Cohn Livingston

Gooseberry Juiceberry

Gooseberry,
Juiceberry,
Loose berry jam.

Spread it on crackers,
Spread it on bread,
Try not to spread it
Onto your head.

Gooseberry,
Juiceberry,
Loose berry jam.

No matter how neatly
You try to bite in,
It runs like a river
Down to your chin.

Gooseberry,
Juiceberry,
Loose berry jam.

Eve Merriam

Ice Cream

Melting, it
Softly fills
The mouth

With something
Like the velvet
Word *vanilla*.
Valerie Worth

Baby's Drinking Song

    Sip a little
Sup a little
    From your little
Cup a little
    Sup a little
Sip a little
    Put it to your
Lip a little
    Tip a little
Tap a little
    Not into your
Lap or it'll
    Drip a little
Drop a little
    On the table
Top a little.

    James Kirkup

Meg's Egg

Meg
Likes
A *reg*ular egg
Not a poached
Or a fried
But a *reg*ular egg
Not a deviled
Or coddled
Or scrambled
Or boiled
But an *egg*ular
*Meg*ular
*Reg*ular
Egg!
Mary Ann Hoberman

Spaghetti! Spaghetti!

Spaghetti! spaghetti!
You're wonderful stuff,
I love you spaghetti,
I can't get enough.
You're covered with sauce
and you're sprinkled with cheese,
spaghetti! spaghetti!
oh, give me some please.

Spaghetti! spaghetti!
piled high in a mound,
you wiggle, you wriggle,
you squiggle around.
There's slurpy spaghetti
all over my plate,
spaghetti! spaghetti!
I think you are great.

Spaghetti! spaghetti!
I love you a lot,
you're slishy, you're sloshy,
delicious and hot.
I gobble you down
oh, I can't get enough,
spaghetti! spaghetti!
you're wonderful stuff.

Jack Prelutsky

WELL, WOULD YOU?—

I Wouldn't

There's a mouse house
In the hall wall
With a small door
By the hall floor
Where the fat cat
Sits all day,
Sits that way
Every day
Just to say,
"Come out and play"
To the nice mice
In the hall wall
With the small door
By the hall floor.

And do they
Come out and play
When the fat cat
Asks them to?

Well, would you?

John Ciardi

Cats and Dogs

Some like cats, and some like dogs,
and both of course are nice
if cats and dogs are what you want
 — but I myself like mice.

For dogs chase cats, and cats chase rats
I guess they think it's fun.
I like my mouse the most because
he won't chase anyone.

N. M. Bodecker

Goldfish

I have four fish with poppy eyes.
Awfully poppy for their size, —
Perhaps they're poppy from surprise;

For after frisking in a sea,
Fish must find it queer to be
Looking through a glass at ME.

Aileen Fisher

Rabbit and Lark

"Under the ground
　　It's rumbly and dark
and interesting,"
　　Said Rabbit to Lark.

Said Lark to Rabbit,
　　"Up in the sky
There's plenty of room
　　And it's airy and high."

"Under the ground
　　It's warm and dry.
Won't you live with me?"
　　Was Rabbit's reply.

"The air's so sunny.
　　I wish you'd agree,"
Said the little Lark,
　　"To live with me."

But under the ground
　　And up in the sky,
Larks can't burrow
　　Nor rabbits fly.

So Skylark over
　　And Rabbit under
They had to settle
　　To live asunder.

And often these two friends
　　Meet with a will
For a chat together
　　On top of the hill.

James Reeves

This Big Cat

This big cat
when small
a shoebox was
his favorite place
of all.

Now
he's old and big and fat.
But no one's ever told him
that
he can no longer fit
inside of it
and so he tries.

He gets his
head
and two big paws
inside
purrs
closes his eyes
and dreams.

It seems
to
him
he hasn't changed at all.
Beatrice Schenk de Regniers

A Cat Is

soft and warm, and sings,
and likes to play with twisty things
like yarn and strings
or bouncy balls.
He also thinks bare trees are nice,
especially if they move like mice.

It's safer, when he wants to play,
to keep your shoes on
(at least partway),
and offer him some other toy
instead of you.
A leaf, or just a shadow,
will do.

Adrien Stoutenburg

To Sup Like a Pup

To sup
Like a pup,
To gulp it all up
No napkin
No fork
No spoon
And no cup
But to slup
With your tongue
In dee-lish-able laps . . .
What luck!

Dorothy Baruch

As I Was Going Along—

As I Was Going Along

As I was going along, along,
A-singing a comical song, song, song,
The lane that I went was so long, long, long,
And the song that I sang was so long, long, long,
And so I went singing along.

Mother Goose

Subway

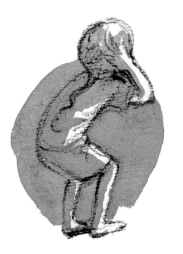

Here come tiger down the track
ROAR-O
Big white eye and a mile-long back
ROAR-O
Through the darkest cave he run
ROAR-O
Never see the sky or sun
ROAR-O

Lillian Morrison

Merry-Go-Round

Horses in front of me,
Horses behind,
But mine is the best one,
He never looks down.
He rises and falls
As if there were waves,
But he never goes under,
Oh, music, oh, mine.

He is steady and strong,
And he knows I am here,
He says he is glad
That I picked him to ride.
But he hasn't a name.
I told him my own,
And he only went faster,
Oh, music, oh, mine.

Around and around,
And the people out there
Don't notice how happy
I am, I am.
The others are too,
But I am the most,
The most, the most,
Oh, music, oh, mine.

Mark Van Doren

Lessie

When my friend Lessie runs she runs so fast
I can hardly see her feet touch the ground
She runs faster than a leaf flies
She pushes her knees up and down, up and down
She closes her hands and swings her arms
She opens her mouth and tastes the wind
Her coat flies out behind her
When Lessie runs she runs so fast that
Sometimes she falls down
But she gets right up and brushes her knees
And runs again as fast as she can
Past red houses
      and parked cars
      and bicycles
      and sleeping dogs
      and cartwheeling girls
      and wrestling boys
      and Mr. Taylor's record store
All the way to the corner
To meet her mama

Eloise Greenfield

Whenever

Whenever I want my room to move,
I give myself a twirl
And busily, dizzily whiz about
In a reeling, wheeling whirl.
Then I spin in a circle as fast as I can
Till my head is weak from churning
Like a tipsy top . . .
And then I stop.
        But my room goes right on turning.
                Mary Ann Hoberman

When I Was Lost

Underneath my belt
My stomach was a stone.
Sinking was the way I felt.
And hollow.
And Alone.

Dorothy Aldis

Did You Ever Have a Dog?

Did you ever have a dog?
I did.
And did it die?
Mine did.
And did you cry?
I did.

And do you know you never will
See him again alive and well?
I do.
But do you dream about him still
And love him more than you can tell?
I do.

Beatrice Schenk de Regniers

40

THE NIGHT IS LONG
BUT FUR IS DEEP—

Grandpa Bear's Lullaby

The night is long
But fur is deep.
You will be warm
In winter sleep.

The food is gone
But dreams are sweet
And they will be
Your winter meat.

The cave is dark
But dreams are bright
And they will serve
As winter light.

Sleep, my little cubs, sleep.

Jane Yolen

At Night

When night is dark
my cat is wise
to light the lanterns
in his eyes.

Aileen Fisher

Snow in the East

Snow in the east,
snow in the west,
snow on my eyelashes
I like best.

Grass in the east,
grass in the west,
grass on my knee bones
I like best.

Rain in the east,
rain in the west,
rain on my bare feet
I like best.

Light in the east,
light in the west,
light in my window
I like best.

Night in the east,
night in the west,
night in my own bed
I like best.

Eve Merriam

Magic Story for Falling Asleep

When the last giant came out of his cave
and his bones turned into the mountain
and his clothes turned into the flowers,

nothing was left but his tooth
which my dad took home in his truck
which my granddad carved into a bed

which my mom tucks me into at night
when I dream of the last giant
when I fall asleep on the mountain.

Nancy Willard

Waking

My secret way of waking
is like a place
to hide.
I'm very still,
my eyes are shut.
They all think I am sleeping
but
I'm wide awake inside.

They all think I am sleeping
but
I'm wiggling my toes.
I feel sun-fingers
on my cheek.
I hear voices whisper-speak.
I squeeze my eyes
to keep them shut
so they will think I'm sleeping
BUT
I'm really wide awake inside
— and no one knows!

Lilian Moore

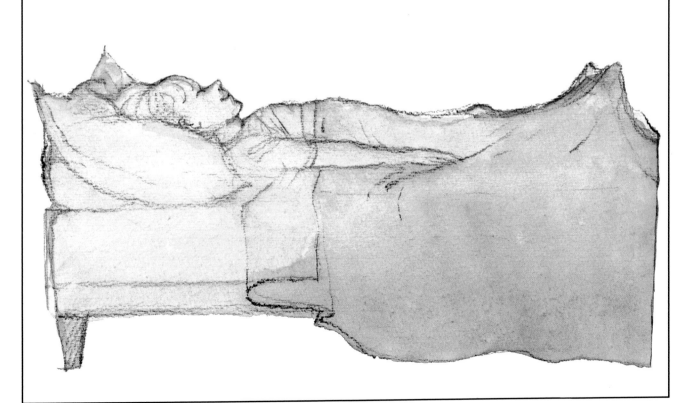

Mother Cat's Purr

Sleep the half-sleep,
Kittens dear,
While your mother
Cat-naps near.

Every kitten
Is a cat,
And you must
Remember that

Naps for cats
Are mostly fake:
Any time
Is time to wake,

Or time to pounce,
Or time to scat.
That's what sleep is —
For a cat.

Jane Yolen

Breathing on the Window Pane in Winter—

The Frost Pane

What's the good of breathing
On the window
Pane
In summer?
You can't make a frost
On the window pane
In summer.
You can't write a
Nalphabet,
You can't draw a
Nelephant;
You can't make a smudge
With your nose
In summer.

Lots of good, breathing
On the window
Pane
In winter.
You can make a frost
On the window pane
In winter.
A white frost, a light frost,
A thick frost, a quick frost,
A write-me-out-a-picture-frost
Across the pane
In winter.

David McCord

Please

Please snow cloud!
Let it flurry.

Make it furry
and thick.

Then catch it,
streets and sidewalks.
Let it stick.

No, snow plow!
Go away.

Please!
Let it stay.

Judith Thurman

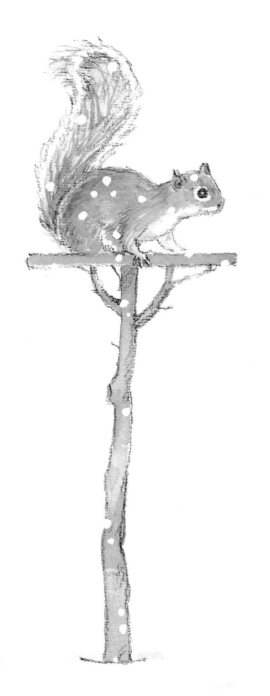

Joe

We feed the birds in winter,
And outside in the snow
We have a tray of many seeds
For many birds of many breeds
And one gray squirrel named Joe.
     But Joe comes early,
     Joe comes late,
     And all the birds
     Must stand and wait.
And waiting there for Joe to go
Is pretty cold work in the snow.

David McCord

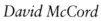

Who Has Seen the Wind?

Who has seen the wind?
　　Neither I nor you:
But when the leaves hang trembling,
　　The wind is passing through.

Who has seen the wind?
　　Neither you nor I:
But when the leaves bow down their heads,
　　The wind is passing by.

Christina Rossetti

Sun

The sun
Is a leaping fire
Too hot
To go near,

But it will still
Lie down
In warm yellow squares
On the floor

Like a flat
Quilt, where
The cat can curl
And purr.

Valerie Worth

Good-by My Winter Suit

Good-by my winter suit,
good-by my hat and boot,
good-by my ear-protecting muffs
and storms that hail and hoot.

Farewell to snow and sleet,
farewell to Cream of Wheat,
farewell to ice-removing salt
and slush around my feet.

Right on! to daffodils,
right on! to whippoorwills,
right on! to chirp-producing eggs
and baby birds and quills.

The day is on the wing,
the kite is on the string,
the sun is where the sun should be —
it's spring all right! It's spring!

N. M. Bodecker

Spring Is

Spring is when
    the morning sputters like
bacon
      and
        your
          sneakers
            run
              down
                the
                  stairs
so fast you can hardly keep up with them,
and
spring is when
    your scrambled eggs
      jump
        off
          the
            plate
and turn into a million daffodils
trembling in the sunshine.

Bobbi Katz

Bright Summer Lives Over the Wall—

I Will Give You the Key

I will give you the key
To this garden gate.
Bright summer
Lives over the wall.
You may play in the sun
Till the season grows late,
And bring back the key in the fall.

Arnold Lobel

From Honey, I Love

The day is hot and icky and the sun sticks to my skin
Mr. Davis turns the hose on, everybody jumps right in
The water stings my stomach and I feel so nice and cool
Honey, let me tell you that I LOVE a flying pool
    I love to feel a flying pool . . .

Eloise Greenfield

Song of Summer

Here comes a bunny
The first to stray
Out of April
And into May.

And here comes a robin
The first to fly
Out of June
And into July.

Here are the fireflies
Last to remember
The end of August
And first of September.

And here comes a caterpillar
The last to creep
Out of summer
And into sleep.

Margaret Wise Brown

Fields of Corn

A kernel of corn!
A kernel of corn!
Plant the kernel,
Let it grow!
Let it grow
Until it bears
An ear of corn.
An ear of corn!
Now there are seeds
And seeds to sow —
Enough to plant
A long, long row.
A row of corn!
A row of corn!
That's how a field
Of corn
Is born.

Sam Reavin

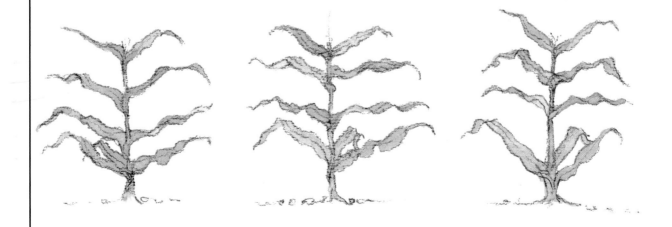

Mine

I made a sand castle.
In rolled the sea.
> "All sand castles
> belong to me —
> to me,"

said the sea.

I dug sand tunnels.
In flowed the sea.
> "All sand tunnels
> belong to me —
> to me,"

said the sea.

I saw my sand pail floating free.
I ran and snatched it from the sea.
> "My sand pail
> belongs to me —
> to ME!"

Lilian Moore

Seaweed

Seaweed from high tide
where sand and breakers meet
gummy
on my tummy,
slippery
on my feet.

Myra Cohn Livingston

Sitting in the Sand

Sitting in the sand and the sea comes up
So you put your hands together
And you use them like a cup
And you dip them in the water
With a scooping kind of motion
And before the sea goes out again
You have a sip of ocean.

Karla Kuskin

Five

Five little children,
Hand in hand,
Went to dig
The yellow sand.

Five little castles,
Trim and neat,
Soon were standing
At their feet.

Five little starfish
Standing near,
Said, "Five little houses! —
Let's live here!"

Claire Tringress

7 Wonder Who Is Coming—

Granny

We've a great big knocker
On the middle of our door,
A lion-headed knocker
With a lion-headed roar;
And when I hear the knocker
As loud as it can be
I wonder who is coming
To see me, me, me.

Is my granny coming?
Is my granny coming?
Is my granny coming
To the door, door, door?

Who is that that's knocking
With a lion-headed roar?
Who lifts up the knocker
And drops it on his head,
His lion-headed, lion-headed
Big brass head?

Is my granny knocking?
Is my granny knocking?
Is my granny knocking
With a lion-headed roar?

Open up the door!
Open up the door!
I hope it is my granny
Who's been knocking at my door!

Patricia Hubbell

Brother

I had a little brother
And I brought him to my mother
And I said I want another
Little brother for a change.

But she said don't be a bother
So I took him to my father
And I said this little bother
Of a brother's very strange.

But he said one little brother
Is exactly like another
And every little brother
Misbehaves a bit he said.

So I took the little brother
From my mother and my father
And I put the little bother
Of a brother back to bed.

Mary Ann Hoberman

Sneeze

There's a
sort of a
tickle
the size of a
nickel,
a bit like the
prickle
of sweet-sour
pickle;

it's a
quivery
shiver
the shape of a
sliver,
like eels in a
river;

a kind of a
wiggle
that starts as a
jiggle
and joggles
its way to a
tease,

which I
cannot
suppress
any longer,
I guess,
so pardon me,
please,
while I
sneeze.

Maxine Kumin

A Kiss Is Round

Round is the moon
When it's bright and full,
Round is a ball
Of knitting wool,
A kiss is round,
And so is a hug;
The rim of a glass,
And the lid of a jug;
The top of a hole
When it's carefully dug.

Blossom Budney

Aunt Roberta

What do people think about
When they sit and dream
All wrapped up in quiet
     and old sweaters
And don't even hear me 'til I
Slam the door?

Eloise Greenfield

Hug o' War

I will not play at tug o' war,
I'd rather play at hug o' war,
Where everyone hugs
Instead of tugs,
Where everyone giggles
And rolls on the rug,
Where everyone kisses,
And everyone grins,
And everyone cuddles,
And everyone wins.

Shel Silverstein

grandpa in march

goes around
    the house
      each
       day

and feels the
    ground
and pinches

      twigs
and   digs
and   digs

pushing
spring

Arnold Adoff

FRANKS WITH BEANS.
KINGS WITH QUEENS—

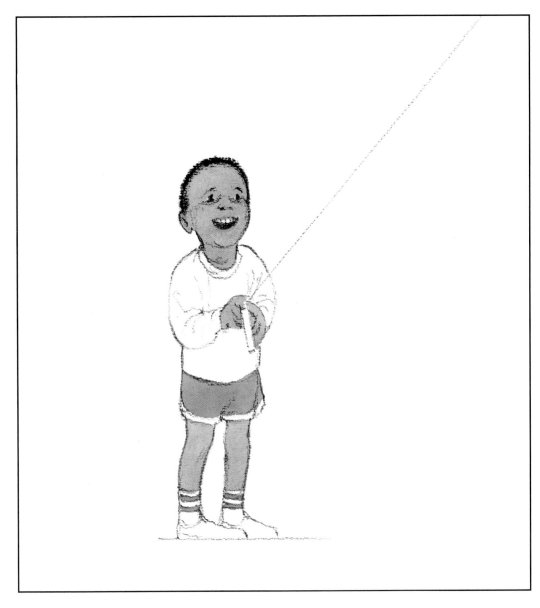

From Some Things Go Together

Hats with heads
Pillows with beds

Franks with beans
Kings with queens

Lions with zoo
and me with you

White with snow
Wind with blow

Moon with night
Sun with light

Sky with blue
AND ME WITH YOU!

Charlotte Zolotow

Cogs and Gears and Wheels and Springs

Inside our mantel clock
are shiny metal things:
cogs and gears and wheels and springs,
with tiny teeth that click

and metal wings that whir and spin,
and seem to sing.

Dad says our clock ticks off the years.
But I don't see how cogs and gears
can make me older by a day
or make my grandma's hair turn gray.

I don't see how wheels and springs
   can click-the-seconds
     into minutes
   whir-the-hours
     into days.

Yet solid on the mantel;
metal heartbeat calm and clear,

   cogs and wheels
   springs and gears

   cogs and wheels
   springs and gears are

ticking seconds into years.

Jacqueline Sweeney

Soap

New cakes of soap
have names you can feel —
letters that stand up under fingers
like ears, lips, eyelids
on a soft face.

Old cakes of soap
are as smooth to stroke
as a chin.

Judith Thurman

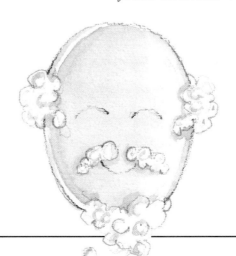

71

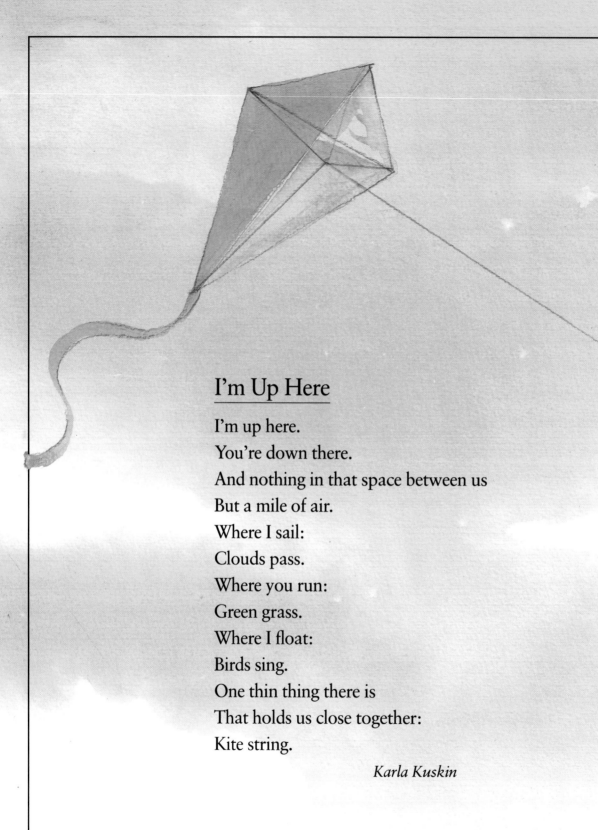

I'm Up Here

I'm up here.
You're down there.
And nothing in that space between us
But a mile of air.
Where I sail:
Clouds pass.
Where you run:
Green grass.
Where I float:
Birds sing.
One thin thing there is
That holds us close together:
Kite string.

Karla Kuskin

September Is

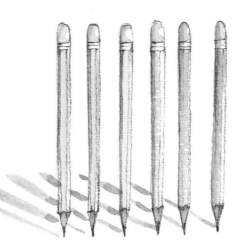

September is
when yellow pencils
in brand new eraser hats
bravely wait on perfect points —
ready to march across miles of lines
in empty notebooks —
and
September is
when a piece of chalk
skates across the board —
swirling and looping —
until it spells your new teacher's
name.

Bobbi Katz

Lunchbox

They always
End up
Fighting —

The soft
Square
Sandwich,

The round
Heavy
Apple.

Valerie Worth

OH WILL YOU BE MY WALLABY?—

The Kangaroo's Courtship

"Oh will you be my wallaby?"
Asked Mr. Kangaroo.
"For we could find so very many
Jumping things to do.
I have a pocket two feet wide
And deep inside,
My dear, you'd ride —
Oh, come and be my bouncing bride,
My valentine, my side-by-side,
I am in love with you."

Jane Yolen

The Light-House-Keeper's White-Mouse

As I rowed out to the light-house
For a cup of tea one day,
I came on a very wet white-mouse
Out swimming in the bay.

"If you are for the light-house,"
Said he, "I'm glad we met.
I'm the light-house-keeper's white-mouse,
And I fear I'm getting wet."

"O light-house-keeper's white-mouse,
I am rowing out for tea
With the keeper in his light-house.
Let me pull you in with me."

So I gave an oar to the white-mouse.
And I pulled on the other.
And we all had tea at the light-house
With the keeper and his mother.

John Ciardi

An Old Person of Ware

There was an old person of Ware,
Who rode on the back of a bear:
When they asked, "Does it trot?"
He said, "Certainly not!
He's a Moppsikon Floppsikon bear!"

Edward Lear

There Once Was a Puffin

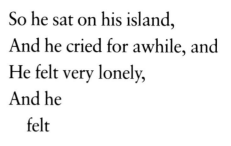

Oh, there once was a Puffin
Just the shape of a muffin,
And he lived on an island
In the
    bright
      blue
        sea!

So he sat on his island,
And he cried for awhile, and
He felt very lonely,
And he
    felt
      very
        small.

He ate little fishes,
That were most delicious,
And he had them for supper
And he
    had
      them
        for tea.

Then along came the fishes
And they said, "If you wishes
You can have us for playmates
Instead
    of
      for
        tea!"

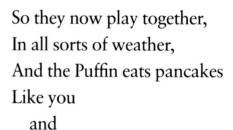

But this poor little Puffin,
He couldn't play nothin',
For he hadn't anybody
To
    play
      with
        at all.

So they now play together,
In all sorts of weather,
And the Puffin eats pancakes
Like you
    and
      like
        me.

Florence Page Jacque

80

If Sunlight Fell Like Snowflakes—

Sunflakes

If sunlight fell like snowflakes,
gleaming yellow and so bright,
we could build a sunman,
we could have a sunball fight,
we could watch the sunflakes
drifting in the sky.
We could go sleighing
in the middle of July
through sundrifts and sunbanks,
we could ride a sunmobile,
and we could touch sunflakes —
I wonder how they'd feel.

Frank Asch

Wouldn't You?

If I
Could go
As high
And low
As the wind
As the wind
As the wind
Can blow —

I'd go!

John Ciardi

If I Were a Snail

If I were a snail
carrying my house
on my back in the rain,
I would move
next door to you,
so I could see you
every day.

Kazue Mizumura

If You Find a Little Feather

If you find a little feather,
a little white feather,
a soft and tickly feather,
    it's for you.

A feather is a letter
from a bird,
and it says,
"Think of me.
Do not forget me.
Remember me always.
Remember me forever.
Or remember me
at least
until
the little feather
is
lost."

So . . .

. . . if you find a little feather,
a little white feather,
a soft and tickly feather,
    it's for you.
    Pick it up
       and . . .
          put it in your pocket!

Beatrice Schenk de Regniers

From If I Were Smaller Than I Am

If I were smaller than I am;
small as a turtle,

I'd give rides to ladybugs,
and listen to the patter of raindrops
snug inside my helmet home.

If I were smaller than I am;
small as a squirrel,

I'd live inside the hollow trunk
of an apartment tree.
I'd play baseball with the acorns,
hide and seek among the leaves,
and take long naps stretched out upon
my tree limb balcony.

If I were smaller than I am;
small as a kitten,

my fence could be a castle wall
and I would walk it twice around
before I'd leap the night air to the roof
and stare into the window
of the queen.

Jacqueline Sweeney

Tree

If only I could stand
still enough, long enough,
with my arms in the air,
I'm sure I could become
a tree.
After a while my fingers would turn green
and my toes would turn down into the ground.
Everyday I'd drink the sunlight
and taste the earth,
but then one day I'd scream,
"Hey, it's me!"
and I'd tell everyone
just what it was like to be
a tree.

Frank Asch

INDEXES

Author Index

TITLE INDEX

FIRST LINE INDEX

ACKNOWLEDGMENTS

ARNOLD ADOFF. "grandpa in march" from *Make a Circle Keep Us In* by Arnold Adoff. Text copyright © 1975 by Arnold Adoff. Used by permission of Bantam Books, a division of Bantam Doubleday Dell Publishing Group, Inc.

DOROTHY ALDIS. "When I Was Lost" from *All Together* by Dorothy Aldis. Text copyright 1925–1928, 1934, 1939, 1952, copyright © 1953–1956, 1962 by Dorothy Aldis. Reprinted by permission of G. P. Putnam's Sons.

FRANK ASCH. "Puddles," "Sunflakes," and "Tree" from *Country Pie* by Frank Asch. Text copyright © 1979 by Frank Asch. Reprinted by permission of Greenwillow Books, a division of William Morrow & Co., Inc.

DOROTHY BARUCH. "To Sup Like a Pup" from *I Would Like to Be a Pony* by Dorothy Baruch. Text copyright © 1959 by Dorothy W. Baruch. Reprinted by permission of Bertha Klausner International Literary Agency, Inc.

N. M. BODECKER. "Cats and Dogs" from *Snowman Sniffles and Other Verse* by N. M. Bodecker. Copyright © 1983 by N. M. Bodecker. "Good-By My Winter Suit" from *Hurry, Hurry, Mary Dear!* by N. M. Bodecker. Copyright © 1976 by N. M. Bodecker. Both are reprinted with permission of Margaret K. McElderry Books, an imprint of Macmillan Publishing Company.

MARGARET WISE BROWN. "Song of Summer" and "Song of the Bugs" from *Nibble, Nibble* by Margaret Wise Brown. Text copyright © 1959 by William R. Scott, Inc. Renewed 1987 by Roberta Brown Rauch. Reprinted by permission of HarperCollins Publishers.

BLOSSOM BUDNEY. "A Kiss is Round" from *A Kiss Is Round* by Blossom Budney. Copyright © 1954 by Lothrop, Lee & Shepard Company. Copyright renewed © 1982 by Blossom Budney. Reprinted by permission of Lothrop, Lee & Shepard Books, a division of William Morrow & Co., Inc.

JOHN CIARDI. "I Wouldn't," "Wouldn't You?" and "The Light-House-Keeper's White-Mouse" from *You Read to Me, I'll Read to You* by John Ciardi. Text copyright © 1962 by John Ciardi. Reprinted by permission of HarperCollins Publishers.

ELIZABETH COATSWORTH. "Rhyme" from *The Sparrow Bush* by Elizabeth Coatsworth. Copyright © 1966 by Grosset & Dunlap. Reprinted by permission of Grosset & Dunlap, Inc.

BEATRICE SCHENK de REGNIERS. "If You Find a Little Feather" from *Something Special* by Beatrice Schenk de Regniers. Copyright © 1958, 1986 by Beatrice Schenk de Regniers. "This Big Cat" from *This Big Cat and Other Cats I've Known* by Beatrice Schenk de Regniers. Copyright © 1958, 1985, 1986 by Beatrice Schenk de Regniers. Both are reprinted by permission of Marian Reiner for the author. "Did You Ever Have a Dog?" from *A Week In the Life of Best Friends* by Beatrice Schenk de Regniers. Copyright © 1986 by Beatrice Schenk de Regniers. Reprinted by permission of Atheneum Publishers, an imprint of Macmillan Publishing Company.